I0084533

New Tools for Collaboration

The Experience of the U.S. Intelligence Community

AUTHOR
Gregory F. Treverton

January 2016

A Report of the CSIS Strategic Technologies Program

CSIS | CENTER FOR STRATEGIC &
INTERNATIONAL STUDIES

ROWMAN &
LITTLEFIELD

Lanham • Boulder • New York • London

About CSIS

For over 50 years, the Center for Strategic and International Studies (CSIS) has worked to develop solutions to the world's greatest policy challenges. Today, CSIS scholars are providing strategic insights and bipartisan policy solutions to help decisionmakers chart a course toward a better world.

CSIS is a nonprofit organization headquartered in Washington, D.C. The Center's 220 full-time staff and large network of affiliated scholars conduct research and analysis and develop policy initiatives that look into the future and anticipate change.

Founded at the height of the Cold War by David M. Abshire and Admiral Arleigh Burke, CSIS was dedicated to finding ways to sustain American prominence and prosperity as a force for good in the world. Since 1962, CSIS has become one of the world's preeminent international institutions focused on defense and security; regional stability; and transnational challenges ranging from energy and climate to global health and economic integration.

Thomas J. Pritzker was named chairman of the CSIS Board of Trustees in November 2015. Former U.S. deputy secretary of defense John J. Hamre has served as the Center's president and chief executive officer since 2000.

CSIS does not take specific policy positions; accordingly, all views expressed herein should be understood to be solely those of the author(s).

© 2016 by the Center for Strategic and International Studies. All rights reserved.

ISBN: 978-1-4422-5912-6 (pb); 978-1-4422-5913-3 (eBook)

Center for Strategic & International Studies
1616 Rhode Island Avenue, NW
Washington, DC 20036
202-887-0200 | www.csis.org

Rowman & Littlefield
4501 Forbes Boulevard
Lanham, MD 20706
301-459-3366 | www.rowman.com

Contents

Introduction

It is 2009. A diverse community of U.S. satellite sensor operators, military personnel on watch duty and intelligence analysts is observing the buildup to a foreign weapons test. This virtual team is spread across the globe, and is dispersed also in functions and agencies—including the following:

- NGA (National Geospatial Intelligence Agency);

- NRO (the National Reconnaissance Office), which builds and operates satellites; and

- NSA (National Security Agency), the nation's signals intelligence (SIGINT) agency.

Only a handful work together or have even met face-to-face. Yet every day they all devote a considerable portion of their busy hours to an Instant Messaging (IM) chat room named "GlobalScene." That chat room and other tools for collaboration across agencies reside on *Intelink,* the backbone created by agreement between the Pentagon and the Intelligence Community in 1994 after the first Gulf War, which hosts versions of tools at all three levels of classification—unclassified, secret and top secret.

As facts change, new clues appear, and possible patterns emerge, this deceptively simple forum, dubbed "CollabZones," helps the participants to maintain and enhance situation awareness.[1] The chat room is a self-organizing conversation that spans technical specialties and organizational boundaries. Some individuals act as "brokers," using their security training to appropriately move information to and fro across their organizational boundaries. Others are "facilitators" trained by the Office of the Director of National Intelligence (ODNI) who specialize in welcoming newcomers and encouraging engagement. News is posted, questions are posed, and unofficial opinions offered. Participants monitor many dozens of other topical and regional chat rooms across different levels of classification, quoting and making reference to relevant postings.

Other social media technologies, all developed in the past decade, are incorporated into the dialogue through hyperlinks and passing mentions. Formal analytic products and briefings are posted on Intelink. An Intellipedia wiki is continuously updated with a timeline and links to various teams, portals and documents. eChirp, a variant of Twitter, is used to broadcast quick updates. GlobalScene is crowdsourcing, spontaneously relating, discovering and discussing across the hidden realms of the U.S. Intelligence Community.

Of all the collaborative instances encountered in preparing this paper, CollabZones is the one most suggestive for the future. In using collaborative tools in combination, the key is a cohesive team, one whose members describe themselves as "agency agnostic." In their work, collaboration is necessary and produces a better "product." Yet the product, or better said,

---

1.   For security reasons, the facility that is the focal point of the Zone cannot be identified in this paper. In any case, the collaboration is very much virtual, with the facilitators often unaware of the locations of participants.

Abbreviations and Terms of Art

AIS	Office of Analytic Integrity and Standards, ODNI
CIA	Central Intelligence Agency
CWE	Common Work Environment, CIA's internal classified network
DI	Directorate of Intelligence, CIA and Defense Intelligence Agency
DIA	Defense Intelligence Agency
DNI, ODNI	Director of National Intelligence, Office of DNI
FBINet	FBI's internal classified network
Five Eyes	United States, Britain, Canada, Australia and New Zealand
G	Gamma, control system for signals intelligence
HCS	HUMINT Control System, control system for human intelligence or espionage
IC	Intelligence Community, the 16 U.S. intelligence agencies considered as an enterprise
ICITE	Intelligence Community IT Enterprise
JWICS	Joint Worldwide Intelligence Communications System, interconnected computer networks operating at the SCI level
NGA	National Geospatial Intelligence Agency
NIC	National Intelligence Council
NOFORN	Distribution to non-US citizens is prohibited, regardless of clearance
NSA	National Security Agency
NSANet	NSA's internal classified network
ORCON	Originator controlled, formally Dissemination and Extraction of Information Controlled by Originator
PDB	President's Daily Brief
PKIs	Public Key Infrastructure certificates, a form of access control beyond classification, providing authentication of a user
SCI	Sensitive compartmented information, methods for handling sensitive intelligence information
SIPRNet	Secret Internet Protocol Router Network, secret-level network widely used by the U.S. military
URL	Uniform Resource Locator, a character stream that constitutes a reference to a specific web resource
WIRe	World Intelligence Review, CIA's daily "publication," now produced only online

output of their work—better situation awareness among a group of analysts—cuts across the way U.S. intelligence traditionally has thought of its work. That traditional process is stove-piped, branded and linear. Its goal is "finished intelligence," words on paper or bytes on a screen that have passed through several layers of management review.

This paper draws on but reshapes the results of a project done for the Center for the Study of Intelligence.[2] This portion of the project was sponsored by the IBM Center for The Business of Government, and is intended for an audience beyond the U.S. Intelligence Community—senior managers in government, their advisors and students of government performance who are interested in the progress of collaboration in a difficult environment. The purpose of this project was to learn lessons by looking at the use of *internal* collaborative tools across the Intelligence Community (IC), especially across the four biggest agencies:

- CIA (Central Intelligence Agency);

- DIA (Defense Intelligence Agency);

- NSA (National Security Agency) and

- NGA (National Geospatial Intelligence Agency).

The initial rubric was tools, but the real focus is collaboration, for while the tools can enable, *what ultimately matters are policies and practices interacting with organizational culture.* It looks for good practices to emulate. The ultimate question is how and how much could, and should, collaborative tools foster integration across the Community. The focus is analysis and the analytic process, but collaborative tools can and do serve many other functions in the Intelligence Community—from improving logistics or human resources, to better connecting collection and analysis, to assisting administration and development, to facilitating, as one interlocutor put it, operational "go" decisions. Yet it is in the analytic realm that collaboration is both most visible and most rubs against traditional work processes that are not widely collaborative.

The study drew on existing literature, especially in looking comparatively at private sector experiences. It made use of available data, especially on Intelink—the suite of tools that is available *across* the various agencies—and on data provided to us by those who manage the tools. Colleagues inside agencies were good enough to post surveys for the project, and those results are reported in the paper. Since those surveys were themselves posted on collaborative tools, respondents were likely to be enthusiasts about those tools. Working sessions with some 50 officers across the Intelligence Community, often on many occasions, compensated, at least in part. The views of those who do not use new collaborative tools, or who tried once or twice and stopped, were diligently sought. For instance, colleagues in the CIA sent a survey by internal e-mail to members of the analytic methods cells at the Agency as well as to several cohorts of classes at the CIA's Sherman Kent School for Intelligence.

The rest of this section defines terms and discusses concepts, first exploring collaboration and coordination, then defining collaborative tools and social media, then surveying the experience of the private sector. The second section of the report uses those distinctions to sort out the blizzard of collaborative tools that have been created in the various intelligence agencies and across them. The third section outlines the state of collaboration, again both within agencies and across them. The report concludes with findings and recommendations for the Community. The recommendations amount to a continuum of possible actions in making more strategic what is and will continue to be more a bottom-up process of creating and adopting collaborative tools and practices.

---

2.   I thank my colleagues in that earlier venture, but they should be spared blame for any defects in this paper.

Defining Collaboration

Collaboration generally is regarded as positive; the adage "two heads are better than one" reflects that connotation.[3] Yet collaboration also carries costs. It is at least time-consuming. Moreover, it requires humility, for reaching out implies a sense of need. So the first question is: why collaborate? A growing literature focused on productivity reviews the impact of virtual and remote collaboration.[4] Starting with studies of office space layout and the impact of physical distance on collaboration, detailed analyses link work assignments, product features, and team roles.[5] Plainly, working across different, and strong, organizational cultures is a challenge for the Intelligence Community, and outside studies underscore the obstacles of geographic dispersion, electronic dependence, and dynamic structure, all of which limit increases in productivity. The studies underline trust as crucial in mitigating these effects.[6]

Collaboration might be divided into two broad types:

- **Collaboration that is driven by shared interest,** which may or may not later lead to products, is discourse collaboration, and

- **Collaboration on concrete analytical products and reports** is substantive collaboration.

To be sure, the former type of collaboration is more difficult to identify and to measure. For the Intelligence Community, the overarching point is that so long as existing workflows, stovepiped and branded by agency, limit substantive collaboration in pursuit of a specific product, collaboration will be limited to discourse collaboration in communities of interest, in which individuals collaborate out of mutual interest in a topic but not necessarily to solve a specific problem or create a specific product. On Intellipedia, for instance, individuals voluntarily assemble and capture knowledge of broad interest to the community without a problem-specific goal for this knowledge.

It is also important to distinguish "collaboration" from "coordination," all the more so because the latter is a term of art in the IC. There, it means securing the okay from another office or agency before proceeding, usually with the publication of a finished intelligence product. It is a requirement. In contrast with coordination, collaboration is a choice. Indeed, the project's interlocutors report that collaboration sometimes is a tool for coordination: analysts would share and discuss drafts informally with counterparts in other offices or agencies in the hope that the "collaboration" would facilitate coordination, muting complaints from those other units when the time comes for formal coordination.

Collaborative Tools and Social Media

The explosion of social media has fired the interest in new tools for collaboration. But it is worth being careful about terms. Not all collaborative tools are social media, and not all social media are very collaborative. Indeed, "social media" turns out to be not very helpful as a label, for it lumps together a range of applications with overlapping and discrete functions. Of familiar media, for instance, Twitter is highly social: anyone can join. In contrast, Facebook is primarily a means of letting people keep in touch with a network of "friends."

---

3.   Richard J. Hackman, *Collaborative Intelligence: Using Teams to Solve Hard Problems*, (San Francisco: Berrett-Koehler), 2011, pp. 26–27.
4.   Thomas J. Allen, *Managing the Flow of Technology* (Cambridge: MIT Press, 1977).
5.   Carliss Y. Baldwin and Kim B. Clark, "Where Do Transactions Come From? A Network Design Perspective on the Theory of the Firm" (Working Paper, 2006)
6.   Cristina B. Gibson and Jennifer L. Gibbs, "Unpacking the Concept of Virtuality: The effects of geographic dispersion, electronic dependence, dynamic structure, and national diversity on team innovation," *Administrative Science Quarterly* 51 (2006):451–495.

The general term "social media" obscures the discrete functions of individual applications. Moreover, "social" tends to connote non-work purposes.

Figure 1 displays the range of collaborative tools.[7] The horizontal axis describes the size of the user pool, from peer-to-peer communication to tools that are, in principle, open to almost anyone (or in the IC, anyone with the appropriate clearances). The vertical axis in the figure indicates the nature of exchange of information, from basic sharing to active integration intended to create a product. The figure is meant to display the range of tools and purposes. Many tools can be used for more than one purpose, and so the precise location of any tool could be debated. Microblogs, like Twitter, are most used for simply sharing information, but they can also be used for crowdsourcing to solve a problem, and in that role would be located higher in the figure—that is, more toward content creation.

Figure 1: Collaborative Tools

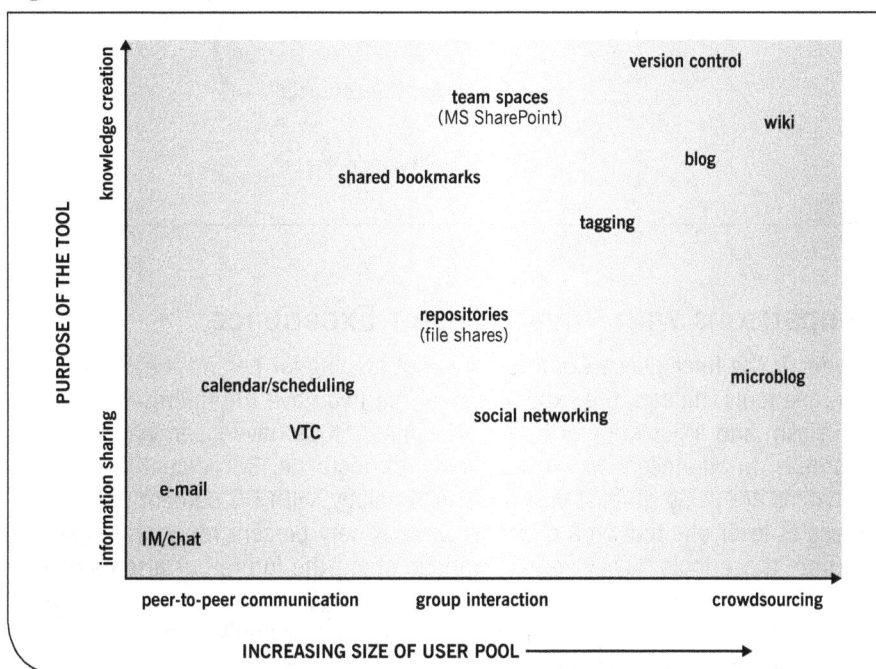

In Figure 2, the sizes of the ellipses reflect the relative numbers of types of connections between people, from a large pool of "unlikely contacts" to a core of close ties. The social media in each ellipse are those most relevant to enabling collaboration within ellipses and from outer to inner ellipses.[8]

The tools in the outermost ring are most powerful as collaborative tools by collectively engaging individuals who may never know one another. In contrast, if close ties use social networking tools, they do so only for preference or convenience; IM or e-mail would serve as well. However, particular social media play roles in more than one of the ellipses. Blogs and microblogs, for example, could also be a way to identify and learn from a fellow specialist without ever meeting. Wikis, like Intellipedia, can be a part of crowdsourcing.

---

7.   *Spotlight: Definition of Collaborative Tools*, Collaborative Tools Strategy, University of California, Berkeley, March 2009, accessed 09 March 2013 (http://technology.berkeley.edu/cio/presentations/ucbcts/ucbcts_spotlight-definition_collaborative_tools.pdf).
8.   Andrew McAfee, *Enterprise 2.0: New Collaborative Tools for Your Organization's Toughest Challenges* (Boston: Harvard Business Press, 2009), 126.

Figure 2: Rings of Contacts and Roles of Social Media in Collaboration

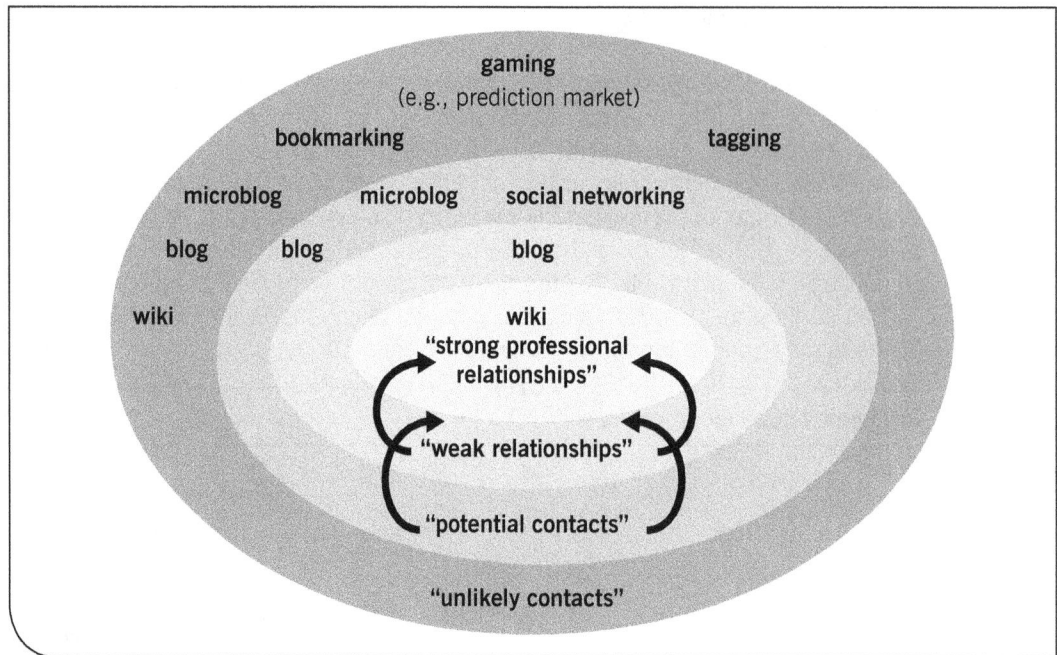

Comparisons with Private Sector Experience

In general, the Intelligence Community is not lagging far behind the private sector in using collaborative tools. Indeed, the experiences of the two have run interestingly in parallel. Early enthusiasm and a flowering of tools in the mid-2000s have given way to a sense of plateau or crossroads. In one recent McKinsey survey, for instance, 83 percent of respondents said their companies are using at least one social technology, with 65 percent noting that their employees use at least one tool on a mobile device. Ninety percent reported reaping measurable benefits from these tools.[9] They were optimistic about the future but also cautious, suggesting that it will be hard to continue to match the early gains. They were also aware of the risks, in the coin of possible leaks of confidential information or intellectual property, but three-fifths believe the gains are worth the risks.

NSA seems the leader in collaboration among the agencies, if largely for internal purposes. NSA is proud of what it's doing. It has the advantage, given its considerable in-house programming capacity, of not needing to count on or wait for outside vendors. The leadership believes that collaboration isn't a duplication of effort but rather a useful combining of different perspectives. It is democratizing problem solving in a way that is a best practice not just for the Intelligence Community but beyond. It is taking risks in the wireless arena that are impressive and counterintuitive for an agency that is among the most security-conscious. And perhaps most interesting (and most in contrast with the other big agencies), NSA is engaging the workforce in designing systems to harvest expertise across the enterprise.

---

9.   "Executives report that the adoption of social media tools at their companies is high—and that this usage could spur additional benefits," McKinsey Global Report, March 2013, available as of April 3, 2013, at https://www.mckinseyquarterly.com/article_print. aspx?L2=4&L3=43&ar=3073.

Collaboration and Trust: Does Collaboration Lead to Greater Productivity?

The private sector's concern over leaks and intellectual property suggests that one apparent advantage of the private sector over intelligence—the latter's constraints of secrecy and compartmentation—should not be overstated. Indeed, one ODNI manager reckoned the balance the other way around: intelligence had an advantage precisely because it had complete control, and thus can monitor users in detail and develop metrics at will. Still, companies have been able to leverage external connections to foster internal collaboration in a way the IC finds difficult. MITRE, for instance, developed tools for the Department of Homeland Security (DHS), then found itself adapting them for use internally.

Collaboration turns on need, and U.S. intelligence organizations are not known for their humility. If they reach out, it is more likely to be regarded as a favor than a necessity. Moreover, knowledge *is* power, and the urge to be first and best with the intelligence drives the community. In that light, sharing increases the circle of those in the know, and thus "sharing" often is reduced to the minimum necessary: analysts may use search tools to locate fellow experts but then take the communication offline, so that both experts can protect their personal and organizational equities.

Moreover, reaching out requires *trust,* which has a special force in the Intelligence Community. "Openness" is one thing if the audience or group is well defined and known. That is almost a paradox: intelligence is open but only in a closed and controlled environment and on a trusted system. In particular agencies, within those confines the group may display amazing "openness," but an unknown quantity—say, someone outside the specified group—raises a fear of the unknown, despite clearances. That is perhaps why Intellipedia has struggled with getting more people to participate. It and any other system that has no access controls opens sharing to people who are by definition unknown, so the amount of openness is severely constricted.

One theme of the business experience with collaborative tools, however, is very suggestive for the IC and clearly recognized by NSA: the tools will not simply bubble up from below. It takes a push from the top. In the words of the 2013 McKinsey review: "To accelerate these changes and make them stick, a growing number of leaders have begun to stress the importance of driving social media skills throughout the organization." In the IC, by contrast, virtually all of the development so far has been bottom-up. There has been little push from the top.

Implementing social media-like applications, "social IT," not only incurs costs for design and integration but also requires an executive-level decision with buy in at successive management levels. Private organizations have managed the accompanying risk by testing the practice with pilot projects and, depending on the success, incrementally adding social-media features to the enterprise system. As examples, Oracle,[10] Pitney Bowes,[11] and Dell[12] each started with CrowdSourcing/Open Innovation by implementing an application to solicit ideas for products or improvements in the company. [13] When the feature was popular and effective, the companies felt comfortable integrating a range of social media. From 2007 to 2009, Oracle began with

10.   Kellsey Ruppel, "The History of Oracle Connect," *Oracle WebCenter Blog,* 13 February 2012, accessed on 10 March 2013 (https://blogs.oracle.com/webcenter/entry/the_history_of_oracle_connect).

11.   Allison Dahl, Jill Lawrence, and Jeff Pierce, "Building an Innovation Community," *Research Technology Management*, September-October 2011, 19–27.

12.   Elizabeth Lupfer, "Dell Uses Social Media to Foster Employee Ideas and Engagement," *The Social Workplace*, 02 October 2009, accessed on 10 March 2013 (http://www.thesocialworkplace.com/2009/10/02/dell-uses-social-media-to-foster-employee-ideas-and-engagement/).

13.   Henry Chesbrough with James Euchner, "The Evolution of Open Innovation: An Interview with Henry Chesbrough," *Research Technology Management*, September-October, 2011.

IdeaFactory and then added social networking in Connect 1.0, discussion groups and a taxonomy of products in Connect 2.0, microblogging in Connect 3.0, and shifted the emphasis to "who is posting, vs. what is posted," in Connect 4.0.

MITRE has a particularly deep history (since 1994) of exploiting the benefits of social media through integration into the enterprise system. MITRE emphasized four keys to effective internal social media:

- Integrate social technology into existing work practices,

- Experiment with social technologies,

- Target early adopters and market successes, and

- Create a social technology platform.[14]

In 2007, in order to better understand the tools' effectiveness, MITRE shifted from statistics on usage to attempting to measure "technology-mediated networks" in order to calibrate the effectiveness of social media features.

Metrics for collaboration are a challenge for both the private sector and U.S. intelligence. NSA has considered, even implemented, some creative incentives to induce people to participate. It has yet to incorporate collaboration as a performance metric but *is* considering how to do so sensibly. It is also developing detailed metrics on tool use—measuring over time which programs are gaining traction and which aren't.

In the private sector, the metrics used to capture productivity improvements from collaborative tools tend to focus on outward-facing interactions. For instance, if a customer misses a flight, she might tweet the airline, and the airline help desk would respond by rerouting her fairly quickly. These external, customer-facing interactions can be measured (time to response, tweet positive/negative emotion levels); however, the internal collaboration (the customer service representative monitoring the Twitter feed, redirecting or alerting the reservations/rebooking office) is more difficult to measure. Because of secrecy, most collaboration in the IC faces inward, indeed is within agencies while cooperation across agencies does resemble the private sector more. Suppose an analyst asks on eChirp "Does anyone know what's going on in Angola right now?" These nominally outward-facing events are really more "inside," linking analysts at different agencies. Capturing the productivity of this interaction requires the more elusive internal collaboration metrics.

Moreover, most of the productivity measures are for individual workers, rather than the productivity or added revenue of the collaborative tool. The most direct measure of productivity, return on investment for new IT services, turns out to be more elusive than might be expected.[15] Both sides of the equation, increases in productivity and costs, are hard to quantify. Suppose a hardware or software upgrade loads applications faster: how does a company measure improved worker satisfaction if Outlook or Firefox only crashes once a day, not four times?

As a result, the productivity measures that get used fall into two camps—direct monetary benefits from time saved by using a collaborative tool, and knowledge accessibility measures using human-computer interaction metrics and social network analysis tools. A recent

---

14. Bill Donaldson, Bala Iyer, Donna Cuomo, and Salvatore Parise, "Mitre Corporation: Using Social Technologies to Get Connected," *Ivey Business Journal,* Strategy, January/February 2011.
15. McAfee, *Enterprise 2.0,* 192.

McKinsey survey of collaborative tool use identified potential productivity increases across internal usage, customers, and partners and suppliers (Table 1).[16]

Table 1: McKinsey's Potential Productivity Impacts from Collaborative Tool Use

Internal	Customers	Partners, Suppliers
• Increasing speed to access knowledge • Reducing communication costs • Reducing travel costs • Increasing speed to access internal experts • Increasing employee satisfaction	• Increasing marketing effectiveness • Increasing customer satisfaction • Reducing marketing costs • Reducing travel costs • Reducing customer-support costs	• Reducing communication costs • Increasing speed to access knowledge • Reducing travel costs • Increasing speed to access internal experts • Increasing satisfaction of partners, suppliers, and external experts

Source: McKinsey Global Survey Results 2013

The other major approach focuses on knowledge access.[17] Some of these involve human-computer interaction metrics, such as "clicks to knowledge"—the number of clicks required to access specialized information on a company intranet. Companies such as MITRE have taken a broader social perspective, trying to see if users of collaborative tools who "brokered" connections among distinct subgroups of workers across the organization tended also to be rated by their managers as highly innovative.

Collaborative Tools in Journalism and Open Source Development

Two private-sector areas are natural points of reference for the Intelligence Community—journalism and open source development, like GitHub. For journalism, though, one big difference is that even the highest quality media now face existential competition from new, mostly web-based sources. To be sure, the IC also feels the competition from outside information sources, but only for NGA does that threat approach existential.

Journalism. The *New York Times* is not a cutting-edge social media practitioner. No wikis, no microblogs, no fancy or modern in-house tool development are apparent. It encourages collaboration but relies on e-mail. Yet all interlocutors at the *Times,* the journalists, editors, and managers, all stressed how fundamentally journalism has changed in the past decade or so:

- **Collaboration** is the name of the game today. Most bylines are multiple authors, often from different locations. This is very different from a decade ago.

- **Speed** has forced the *Times* and its competitors to push to the edge of their comfort zone with regard to accuracy. The *Times* stresses that, perhaps more than its smaller and less established competitors, it must often give more weight to being right than being quick, and as a result often loses out to other media organizations in the race to publish first. Nevertheless, it, too, has seen an increase in its resort to the "correction" page.

---

16. Jacques Bughin and Michael Chui, "Evolution of the Networked Enterprise: Survey Results" McKinsey Global Survey Results, 2013. Accessed July 10, 2013 http://www.mckinsey.com/insights/business_technology/evolution_of_the_networked_enterprise_mckinsey_global_survey_results

17. Bill Donaldson, Bala Iyer, Donna Cuomo, and Salvatore Parise, "Mitre Corporation: Using Social Technologies to Get Connected," *Ivey Business Journal,* Strategy, January/February 2011.

- **Editing on the fly** is imperative in these circumstances.

- **Evaluation, career development, and incentives** have kept pace with the changing nature of the business. The paper takes pains to measure contribution, not just solo bylines, and it values a blog posting that attracts readership as much as a print article on the front page.

- **Changing impact measures** are changing value propositions. Appearing above the fold in the print version of the paper is still regarded the place of honor among journalists, but another enviable distinction is making the *Times* "10 most e-mailed" list.

- **Content/version control** is pervasive and central to the publication process. The ability to track versions, attribute to multiple authors, and control versions aimed at print or e-publication is critically important.

- **Customer knowledge** perhaps most distinguishes the *Times* from the IC. It knows its readership exquisitely, to an extent the IC can only dream about.

Open Source. GitHub is an interesting example of how the open source development model has been extended to include the distributed development of much more than source code. GitHub, founded in 2008, began as a web-based hosting service for open source code development, but it has expanded beyond software. More than 450 of its repositories are described as legislation rather than code.[18] Virtually all of these repositories are unofficial, in the sense that they are not endorsed or used by any government. Many of them, though, are for code that can be used to help display/represent legislation. They are also used as public forums to follow the markups to proposed legislation, and to discuss potential language for legislation.[19]

In addition to the repositories, GitHub also includes social media tools for developing and discussing the contents of a repository. The fundamental tool is the Git revision control system, whose key features include:[20]

- Distributed development,

- Tools for visualizing and navigating a non-linear development history, and

- Authentication (based on cryptography) of the history of changes.

The combination of Git revision control and social media helps developers to see and understand the differences between any two versions of code by visualizing additions and deletions, much like a markup to a Word document. It identifies the author of a version of code and it helps to detect attempts to alter a configuration-controlled version of source code once posted. Using this system, distributed development is possible without requiring any organizational structure to govern the developers.

In intelligence, GitHub could be used to produce finished intelligence and would share features with both Intellipedia and with crowdsourcing. Rather than using a blog or wiki, a GitHub repository might be used to create an intelligence report. Any analyst (or Community official) interested in and able to make a contribution could revise a version of the report with the Git system providing revision control and attribution, while social media enabled ancillary communications among contributors. Management would retain responsibility for declaring which "version" of the intelligence report is authoritative, just as someone has to be in charge of deciding which version of Linux code is the current release.

---

18.   This is the material described in Clay Shirky's June 2012 TED talk (http://www.ted.com/talks/clay_shirky_how_the_internet_will_one_day_transform_government.html).

19.   Alex Howard of O'Reilly Radar describes the motivation for an effort to make the US Code available on GitHub (http://radar.oreilly.com/2012/12/the-united-states-code-is-on-github.html) and how it differs from other online sources of the US Code.

20.   See http://git-scm.com/docs/git.html.

Quality assurance could be done in parallel with the drafting of the report, or on the authoritative version. This model might limit the access of officials on the policy, as opposed to intelligence, side only to the authoritative versions of the report but still let them enter into a dialogue through social media with those contributing to the authoritative version. Unlike the current production process, this model would open the process to contributions from others in the IC, not just those analysts directly managed by the organization responsible for the report. Notice the contrast between GitHub and IC practice. Typically, in the IC an organization is responsible for a topic—for instance, CIA's office that covers the Middle East. Those organizations can be seen as a closed publishing system for finished intelligence reports dealing with that topic. The responsible entity assigns analysts to write reports, and performs quality assurance on the results.

Lessons from the Private Sector. The private sector is not, in general, way out in front of the IC in using collaborative tools. Most private organizations are also in the position of having been through one phase of tool-building and adoption, and are now looking to shape the next phase. Private-sector experience does, however, suggest several pointers for the IC.

- One is the importance of a top-down approach to collaboration, not just assuming it will bubble up from the bottom.

- A second, but one harder for the IC to follow, is using external tools to leverage or complement internal ones.

- Third, and perhaps most important, the experience of the New York Times and, still more, that of GitHub and open access, suggest that collaboration becomes real when it drives changes in work flow and product. The process will become collaborative when the product is.

Collaborative Tools in the Intelligence Community

This section turns from the general categories of tools to the rich diversity of the Intelligence Community's tools. The process of adopting collaborative tools has been bottom up. Individual officers began using the tools because they found them intriguing and useful. Budgetary plenty provided money to create many tools. Indeed, some interlocutors thought the plenty had encouraged agencies to do their own thing, creating their own tools rather than collaborating in the process of creating collaborative tools. What does not yet exist is a strategic view from the perspective of the IC enterprise, neither a central architecture nor much attention by senior agency staff to what kinds of incentives to provide for what kinds of collaboration.

The tools fall into two broad categories:

- **The best-used ones are within agencies**, residing on the particular agency's server and thus not in general accessible to anyone in another intelligence agency. Those tend to fall on the left side of Figure 1 on page 9; they are mostly instant messaging (IM) and thus better ways of conducting peer-to-peer communications, though those tools generally do include some chat and other more widely collaborative functions.

- **The second category is tools used across agencies:** the Intelink set which includes a range of collaborative tools and social media.[21]

Collaborative Tools: Recent History and Functions

Loosely, the recent Intelligence Community history of collaborative tools may be divided into two phases:

- The first, beginning in the 2005 timeframe could, with some exaggeration for emphasis, be characterized as dominated by *tools,* with the second, more recent phase dominated by *mission.* In the first phase, with all the "cool stuff" coming out of the private sector, intelligence was attracted to build its own counterparts. A-Space (where "A" is for "analysts") is perhaps the clearest example. The implicit assumption was that if the tool were interesting enough, people would use it. A-Space's early managers made that assumption explicit by trying to design not necessarily a "destination" but at least a web way-station that officials would want to visit en route elsewhere.

- The second, more recent phase has been driven by *mission*.

Many of the early adopters hoped for a revolution in the traditional process for producing "finished" intelligence analyses, caricatured by one blogger as "collect traffic, write paper, publish,

---

21. Access to the open web varies across agencies. Most CIA analysts, for instance, have what amounts to a separate "box" at their desks and can switch to the open web, albeit one that is "open" only with the constraints the Agency applies. So now, most intelligence officers either stay entirely inside the security firewall or have two unclassified "e-lives"—one at their agencies with the limitations that may entail and another, commercial one at home with open access to the web.

repeat." When the revolution did not dawn, some frustration beset the enthusiasts. The goals of the second phase have been more modest. NSA's Tapioca is perhaps the best example. Its creator sought a virtual counterpart to the physical courtyard that Pixar had constructed. His goal, thus, was "unplanned collaboration," and his animating question from the beginning was "what do I need to do my job here at NSA better?" To that end, where NSA already had tools for particular functions—as it did in looking for expertise—he brought in and embellished the tool. Other officers spoke of weaving the tools into the fabric of the workplace, not thinking of them as interesting add-ons.

Figure 3 draws on the discussion in the introduction and characterizes tools by collaborative function, including both agency-specific tools and the Intelink set. As in Figure 1, the horizontal axis displays the size of the potential pool of users, while the vertical axis reflects purposes, from simple information sharing at the bottom to information integration or content creation at the top. Recognizing, again, that tools can serve more than one purpose, the figure displays the range of tools; again, the precise location of any tool could be debated.

Tools for IM, e-mail and VTC are not social media but do play a crucial role in communication. Social networking tools, such as SpySpace, A-Space, and IC Connect, play a fundamental role

Collaborative Tools in the Intelligence Community

The functions of the tools in the Intelligence Community might be grouped in five categories, again recognizing that the categories cannot be entirely discrete, for most tools serve more than one purpose.

- **Discovery.** NSA's Tapioca Neighborhood function, which locates expertise, is a good example. But chatting (instant messaging, IM) and blogging also can aid discovery. One interlocutor refers to chatting and blogging as the "water cooler" function. Yet even chat can cover a range of purposes—from pure logistics (Can I get a ride home?), to mundane discovery (When is the meeting?) to more substantive discovery (Who knows about x?). So, too, blogs can range from curating (setting down ideas for further analysis later), to crowdsourcing (by inviting others to critique an idea or argument), to discovery (by seeing who responds to a blog or asking a question).

- **Curating, reference, and research.** Here, the signature tool is Intellipedia. Like Wikipedia, it contains pages arranged by topic, which officers can add to or edit, with all the metadata available. People also have their own home pages on Intellipedia. It is a handy, living reference.

- **Managing.** Here, the principal tools are probably IM, chats and blogs, and most of the managing is done through agency-specific tools, for most agencies have their own internal chats and blogs. In principle, though, Intelink chat and blogs could be used to manage projects—from analysis to development—across agencies. Tapioca is suggestive of the possibilities, for NSA makes it available to its "five eyes" international partners (Britain, Canada, New Zealand and Australia).

- **Producing original content.** This has been the ambition for several tools, notably A-Space and Intellipedia. Indeed, Intellipedia's managers regret that the association with Wikipedia induces users to think of Intellipedia only as a living encyclopedia, not a forum for producing original content. And A-Space, now i-Space, is valued more for its discovery function—helping analysts with convergent interests locate each other behind the security wall.

- **Outreach.** Here, the signature example is the WIRe (World Intelligence Review), the CIA's daily "publication" that is no longer published in hard copy, only available online. WIRe uses collaborative tools for outreach. For instance, feeds on eChirp are based on topical groups, and provide notice of thought-provoking or special items.

Figure 3: Intelligence Community Collaborative Tools Include More than Social Media

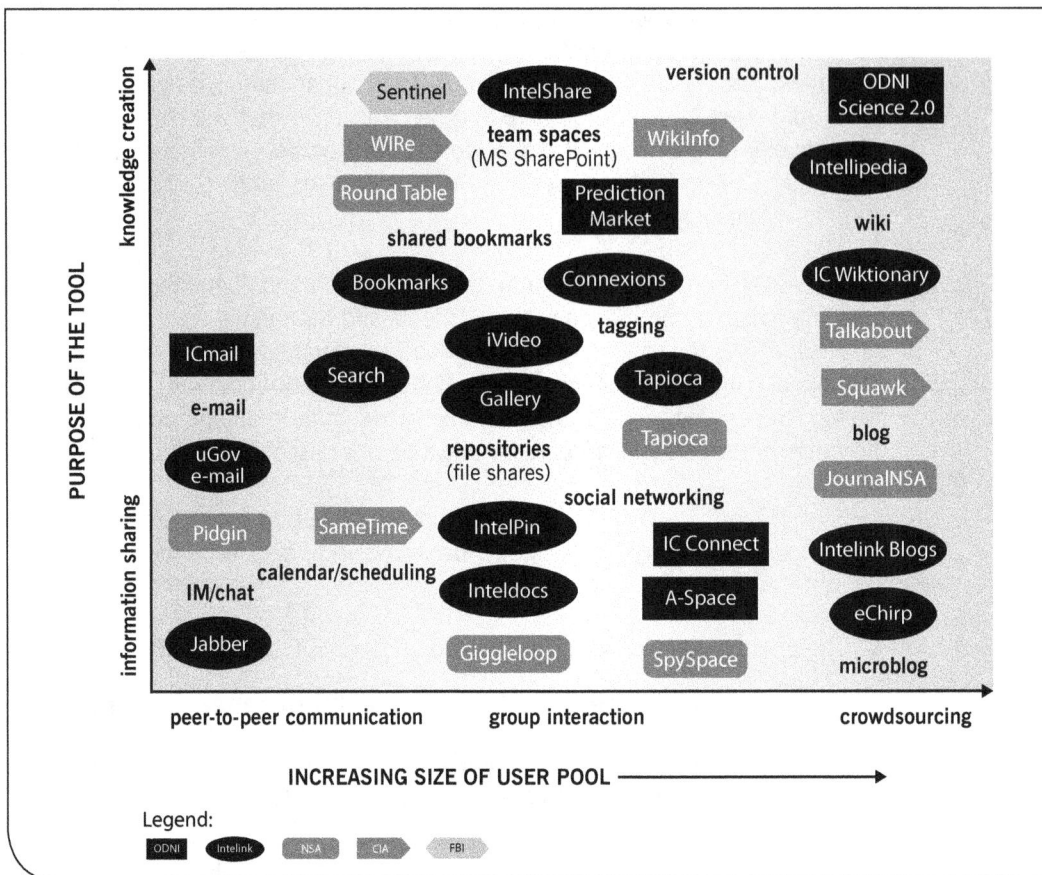

in discourse collaboration by helping experts meet, albeit virtually. Microblogging tools, such as eChirp, further enable discovery of relevant contacts and sharing of ideas. (Note that such tools also allow for peer-to-peer communication.) Tools that span functions, such as Tapioca, hold the potential to increase the ease with which users can discover relevant contacts. Finally, Intelink Search, while not strictly social media, plays a role in discovery of social-media content, such as individual "chirps," which have a unique URL.

Social media also can play a role in substantive collaboration by fostering analysis and dissemination of intelligence. Blogs within agencies and security levels, such as JournalNSA, Talkabout (CIA), and Intelink Blogs, enable spontaneous creation and fluid sharing of information that fosters collaborative analysis, which can ultimately contribute to producing intelligence. Tagging of documents reveals temporal trends (Connexions) in tracking intelligence targets. Other tools help in assessing topics and raise questions of priority, while still others generate predictions (Prediction Market) that may benefit analyses. Wikis, like Intellipedia, have the potential to contribute most directly to the production of an intelligence product by demonstrating the potential for open collaboration in producing content.

Focus on Intelink

Intelink is the backbone for all the Community-wide tools. It was created in the wake of the first Gulf War, in a 1994 agreement between the then-DCI and the deputy secretary of defense. It spans the three domains of classification:

- Unclassified,

- SIPRNet (secret), and

- JWICS (top secret/SCI).

Housed in NSA, it has some 230,000 users across those domains.[22] It provides platforms; it does not curate or get involved in content, though it occasionally will offer advice, for instance on how to make an agency's documents more discoverable. Figure 4 displays the Intelink array of tools, again by size of user pool and most frequent purpose for using the tool; again, any particular tool's location could change depending on the use to which it was put.

Three of the most used tools on Intelink may support collaboration but do not necessarily stimulate it or provide a near real time platform for doing so:

- **Intelink Search** has more than 180 million documents indexed and typically services between two and three million searches per month. [23] A "document" is anything with a unique URL, thus including each individual eChirp, each blog, each item in Inteldocs, Gallery, iVideo, and other tools. This is the classic reference or encyclopedia function, with searchers looking to fill a gap in their knowledge or corroborate information. When Search does not provide the answer, the other collaborative tools may help users broadcast their needs.

- **Inteldocs** tends, in the view of Intelink managers, to get short shrift because it's not so "social." Yet, as a Google Drive or Dropbox-like capability where people can share files, it is absolutely critical to how work gets done. Both Search and Inteldocs reverse the usual pattern of Intelink tools in which JWICS (Joint Worldwide Intelligence Communications

Figure 4: Intelink Tools

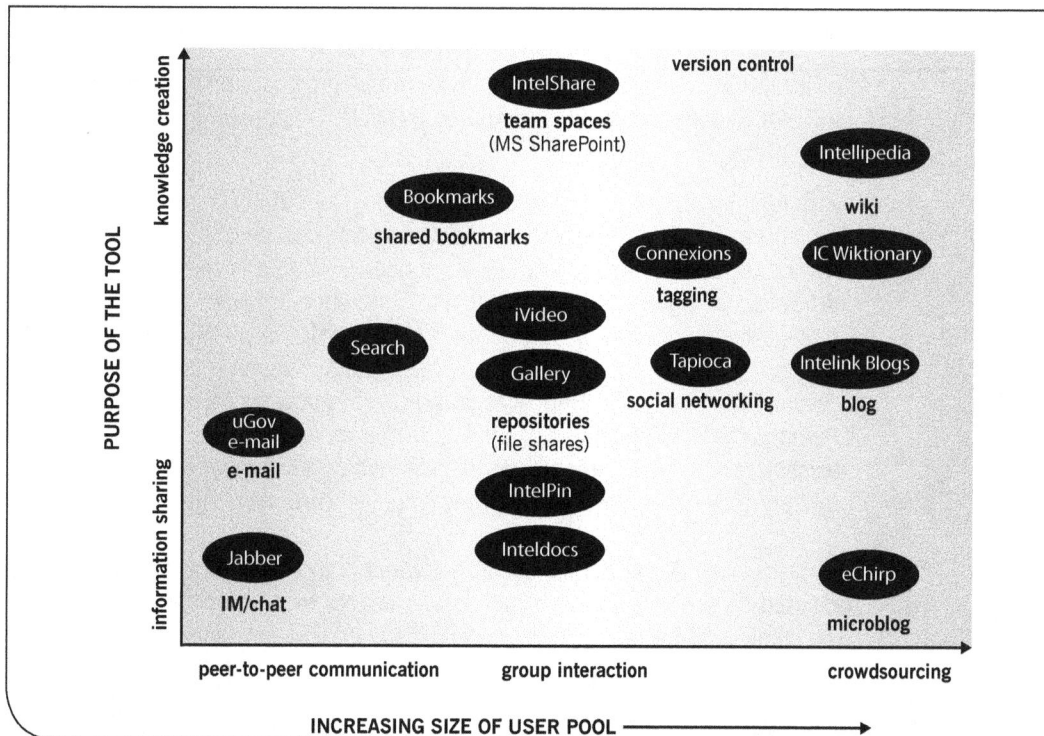

22. No accurate count of the current number of users who are registered with Intelink is available. This estimate is based on log-ins through what are called Passport accounts, the gateway to Intelink.

23. This and other numbers in this section are from https://www.intelink.gov/metrics/dashboard/ices-metrics-by-system.html. The numbers do not yet exist into 2013.

System, interconnected computer networks operating at the SCI level) use trumps that on SIPRNet (secret), which in turn is larger than that at the unclassified level. There have been more than twice as many searches at the SIPR level as at the JWICS level, and while Inteldocs hosts more than two million documents at each of those two levels, it hosts a third more at the SIPR level (JWICS: 1.03 million, SIPR: 1.33 million). Inteldocs usage skyrocketed after the Pentagon tamped down on USB storage usage for transferring files in the wake of the Wikileaks affair.

- **IntelShare or IntelHosting** is the Intelink SharePoint instantiation and is popular judging from the number of sites that are requested and provisioned, which was on the order of 5000 as of September 2012.[24] There are four instantiations—one for Intelink-U, one for Intelink-S and two on the high side, or TS/SCI. One of the latter two is accredited for HCS and G. These are primarily of use to already-defined teams, though Intelink policies try to insist that they be open. The compartmented sites were stood up initially to meet the collaboration needs of the various DNI "mission managers." When teams began to restrict access, Intelink responded that if what the teams sought were "cylinders of excellence," they would have to do that through agency networks. Any new IntelShare sites are to be open. Gallery and iVideo are also repositories for data that may facilitate collaboration.

Four others were designed to be collaborative:

- **Intellipedia**, the oldest of the current tools, began in 2005. It is a multi-purpose system for collaborative data sharing. Like Wikipedia, it is based on MediaWiki. It consists of three wikis, at each of the three levels of classification. As of December 2012, it had 188,000 users at the JWICS level, 147,000 at the SIPR level, and 75,000 at the unclassified level. It is an ever deepening pool of user contributed knowledge.

- **Intelink Blogs** is the inter-agency forum for blogging. It has some 6,000 blogs with 94,000 posts on JWICS since late 2007, compared with 1,300 blogs with 47,000 posts on SIPR or 2,700 blogs with 20,000 posts at the unclassified level, called Intelink-U.[25]

- **eChirp,** the inter-agency Twitter-like microblogging capability, had over 600,000 updates on JWICS since late 2009, compared to 30,000 updates on SIPR and 52,000 updates on Intelink-U.

- **Jabber,** instant messaging, adds value through its utility in meeting mission and providing a platform for situational awareness. It had an average of over 800,000 daily messages in December 2012 at the JWICS level, about 40 times the number at the SIPR level, and 80 times that at the unclassified level. The difference between JWICS and SIPR use is all the more striking because, based on total clearances, the SIPR network is at least twice the size of the JWICS one. For one enthusiast the difference reflects the lack of enough "evangelists" at the SIPR level to communicate how these tools could be leveraged. Perhaps that will change over time, but that too would require users to break out of their existing routines and organizational silos, which are probably at least as rigid in the military as in the civilian parts of the Intelligence Community.

The impressive NSA system for social networking and collaboration, Tapioca, was recently instantiated on Intelink. While it has drawn visitors from a number of agencies, the numbers are too small and the tool too new to draw any conclusion beyond "too early to tell."

---

24. "Instantiate" and "instantiation" are terms of art. Based on the same Latin root as "instance," the term is probably best understood as "installed (or deployed) version." Thus, most agencies use the software SharePoint for team products, but each instantiation is separate, unconnected to others and modified to suit the agency's needs.

25. Here, the metrics stop in December 2011.

Two other tools are important. Both are on JWICS; one is facilitated by Intelink but managed by DIA, the other was created by the DNI's Office of Analytic Integrity and Standards (AIS), later run by the Intelligence Advanced Research Projects Activity (IARPA), and scheduled to move to the National Intelligence Council.

- **A-Space, now i-Space.** Launched in 2008, it, like Intellipedia, is multipurpose, aiming to provide a common collaborative workspace for analysts, with access to databases, the ability to search classified and unclassified sources simultaneously, messaging and other collaborative tools. Based on its being limited to analysts, it was exempted from many originator-controlled, or ORCON, restrictions. It also can carry material classified HCS and G, which Intelink cannot. In July 2013, the long-planned widening of A-Space to i-Space (Integrated Space) finally happened, removing the requirement to be an analyst. That widening was set to go for more than a year but was held up by concerns over spreading the original A-Space exemptions to a much wider community. In the final compromise to widen A-Space to i-Space, the ORCON exemptions were curtailed, limiting publication of ORCON only to closed workspaces.

- **Prediction Market.** The idea stems from observations that financial market traders bet their own money before they offer advice to their clients.[26] In this case, participants make bets by buying or selling contracts that some future event will or won't happen. They buy (go long) if they think the event is likely, sell (go short) if they think it unlikely. If the settlement value of the contract is one dollar if the event occurs and 0 if it doesn't, the contract's current price might be thought of as the probability that the event will occur. While studies have not conclusively shown prediction markets to be better than simpler techniques—like polling experts separately for their probability estimates, then averaging the results—some 80 Community officials participate and are asked about three new questions a week. Not surprisingly, those most enthusiastic about the Prediction Market tended to be those with "hot" accounts involving lots of interesting "Will it or won't it?" questions such as "Will North Korea conduct another nuclear test by date y?"

Inevitably, as the IC's tools were adapted from the world outside government, they lost what is arguably their greatest benefit in the outside world—sheer size. The potential size of the IC user pool is limited—only 4.9 million people hold security clearances of any sort, and only 1.4 million are cleared at the top secret level—and security practices of particular agencies slash that pool further.[27] Actual use of cross-agency tools is much smaller still. For comparison, there have been about three-quarters of a million "chirps" on eChirp, the cross-agency microblog, over the lifetime of the tool, from some 50,000 total users. Twitter has 11,000 times as many users, whose tweets total, *every day,* about 80 times the lifetime total of chirps on eChirp.[28] That lack of scale may contribute to, for instance, the tendency of tools like eChirp to be hijacked for non-work related discussions. To be sure, those tendencies are visible on Twitter as well, but the enormous scale permits people who seek serious conversations to identify people and sources they wouldn't otherwise have known.

---

26. The idea was championed in James Surowiecki, "The Wisdom of Crowds: Why the Many Are Smarter than the Few and How Collective Wisdom Shapes Business," Economies, Societies and Nations (2004).

27. The numbers are from Office of the Director of National Intelligence, *2012 Annual Report on Security Clearance Determinations,* (Washington: ODNI, 2013), available, as of October 22, 3013, at http://www.dni.gov/files/documents/2012%20Report%20on%20 Security%20Clearance%20Determinations%20Final.pdf.

28. The number for eChirp is from the dashboard cited in footnote 11. The Twitter numbers are from http://statisticbrain.com/twitter-statistics/.

The State of Collaboration in the Intelligence Community

The state of collaboration depends on perspective. On the positive side, the agencies and Intelligence Community have been adept at building and adapting tools, and the tools have their devoted users. The IC has come a long way. Even tools that are now taken for granted, like JWICS/Intelink and ICMail (e-mail on JWICS, hence across agencies), represent clear advances in helping officials from different agencies work together. In a few places, most notably NSA, the new tools clearly have the backing of senior management, who are thinking very much in ways similar to the best practices in the private sector about how to provide incentives to drive use deeper into the workforce.

Yet that long way to go is also apparent. The lack of sanctioned senior support or real incentives to use the cross-agency tools came up again and again in the conversations, admittedly most often with the enthusiasts but not contradicted by others. Those enthusiasts tended to regard themselves as a hardy band of adventurers on hostile terrain. As one committed CIA blogger put it: "I'm practically unpromotable." Only one senior officer came up as a user of the cross-agency tools. Instead of getting validation from seniors, many officers have the impression that time spent using collaborative tools is dismissed as "goofing off."

The gap between the use of *intra-agency* tools, primarily for peer-to-peer communication, and the use of *cross-agency* tools was striking. For instance, of 142 CIA respondents to a survey, 140 used SameTime, the CIA IM, *daily*, but 107 had *never* used Jabber, the Intelink IM, and 82 had never used eChirp. Intellipedia is more used, perhaps not surprisingly given that its evangelists sit in the CIA. Only 11 had never used Intellipedia, while 74 only browsed the site. Forty-one respondents have never used Intelink blogs, while 78 have only browsed, not contributed. Ninety-three have never used A-Space, even though it was intended for analysts, and 23 have only browsed; 18 have contributed a time or two but stopped.

This section outlines both the benefits of collaboration across agencies and the obstacles—relying on the project's conversations, blog entries and the results of several surveys posted for us or sent by internal e-mail by colleagues inside the Community. The survey, reproduced in the Appendix, was mostly closed-ended and designed to be completed in less than five minutes. In conclusion, the section returns to CollabZones and several other especially promising initiatives in collaboration.

What Users Find Beneficial

Those who used the cross-agency tools on Intelink cited a handful of reasons for doing so. One was situational awareness. As one Korea specialist puts it, "I look at eChirp first thing in the morning because my colleagues in Korea and Japan have been working while I was sleeping." A second reason is to identify new colleagues around the Community. That same Korea specialist says he hasn't identified a fellow Community expert other than through the collaborative tools in the last five years. One NGA office uses a blog to circulate interim "publications" between more formal ones; in that way, it keeps its community together and its analysts in form. Individual bloggers use the blogs for "warehousing" and seeking comment on items not yet ready for publication. In at least one case, that of CIA's WIRe, the tools are used for "outreach," highlighting items for relevant analytic communities.

Among officers who cite specific examples when collaborative tools had been useful, one cited record keeping, and another cites Intellipedia as better than e-mail or shared drives for recording his or her own information. Another official started an Intellipedia page to document a specific targeting practice. "I managed to get a lot of IC collaboration and we build some robust pages—but as time passed and we moved on to new accounts, those pages became outdated and no one updates them now." Another started using eChirp blogs and a wiki to help spread the word about a new grassroots group. "I have found it interesting, but it seems like most people are NOT using them." Still another's team runs an iSpace page on strategic counterterrorism issues. One says that several officers, all within CIA, had reached out for advice about training in social psychology after having seen his or her Intellipedia page. One interviewee notes when collaborative media *would have* been useful: "There was a post-Arab Spring task force that constructs situation reports. It has little institutional memory. The task force does not see the use of social media as a way to 'do things' in order to create institutional memory. There is no way to capture history. The culture and incentives are missing."

Another officer is very enthusiastic about using the tools for situation awareness, both to quickly get information from people and to "keep up with what is going on in the world," particularly citing the Open Source Center's chat rooms. Still another person says something similar: "People in the government use social media tools to ask awkward questions that challenge the 'common knowledge' of experts on any given subject area. Sometimes these are ignored—but when they are engaged, these discussions can become extremely useful exercises in alternative analysis."

Another respondent finds informal blogs useful "to get a pulse of what others at the agency are thinking ... without obsessing so much about perfect sentence construction and conciseness like we do in other vehicles." Another survey respondent offers the example of getting cross-agency input on a specific budgetary question. He or she uses Intellipedia to document best practices, often getting a question via SameTime or e-mail, then answering by including a link to an informative Intellipedia page. Four others cite Intellipedia as a way to capture a large amount of background information on particular issues.

Obstacles to Use

The obstacles cited by officials range across organizational culture, trust and incentives, as well as classification and practical difficulties.

Obstacle One: Organizational Culture Does Not Encourage Collaboration

As one blogger puts it: "We're still combatting 'stovepipes of excellence.'" This may not be a tools issue, but rather a culture issue. It may require generational change in senior management before we see any fundamental shifts in the way we do collaboration." Another blogger emphasizes competition: "I would offer that at least some of the resistance [to] collaborative assessments is fear of being scooped if they put their assessments out there for the world to see before they are ready to publish. Nobody wants their boss sending them a note on someone else's product asking why some other agency published on 'our' topic before we did. Yes, that should drive innovation and process improvement internally, but not sharing is just simpler."

Another perspective: "The fact that we are trained to not participate in private life makes us conditioned not to participate internally." That reluctance is reinforced by a desire not to be "wrong" and a DI [CIA Directorate of Intelligence] culture that emphasizes speaking with one voice externally, and so discourages internal dissent, particularly when there might be a record of it. The lack of incentives is mentioned often in the interviews, and as one respondent notes "our work processes are linear and hierarchical, rather than group-collaborative. That is especially true across agency boundaries—genuine cross-agency collaboration remains relatively rare."

It might seem that young analysts who are digital natives would extend the connectedness in their personal lives to work. On second thought, though, socialization can be rapid, all the more so if the traditional production culture is strong and thus the incentives to use collaborative tools correspondingly weak. One blogger puts it colorfully:

> It's not generational. In fact, the 'new' employees have been somewhat disappointing in their outlook and expected performance based on extrapolating mostly marketing studies of 'youth' and technology. This isn't a market, it's work and it's much harder to change culture than texting your friends endlessly. If you take a college kid out of Virginia Tech, who is used to blowing off a few classes, drinking and watching football on the weekends, put him in a tie and suit, and tell him he will make more money if he does XYZ, not unmiraculously he's going to start doing XYZ.

Obstacle Two: Lack of Trust among Users
A blogger reports: "With a blog, you may not know the background or the experience, or even the identity of a blog participant. Also, it is not safe to assume that the participants of a blog accurately represent the population working on that issue. People choose to participate in a blog. Knowledgeable people may or may not choose to participate. People with opinions may choose to participate in blogs." An NSA officer comments that "NSANet users are a known quantity, JWICS [Intelink] users (despite the fact that everyone acknowledges the clearances are the same) are not. You can't get in trouble for sharing data that you're not allowed to share if you don't venture away from home."

Obstacle Three: Lack of Incentives to Collaborate
One survey respondent wonders "if the threat [to one's job] presented is a big issue—'If I share this info, someone else will find out and become the expert or they won't need to use my tool/silo anymore or maybe they won't need me.'" Somewhat less dramatically, one respondent offers that occasionally Intellipedia is a good source, "but it is so ill-updated it is rarely more helpful than using either SameTime or the phone to ask a person." One officer had tried a blog on professional development but "found the time invested to bring little return in the way of feedback or having an impact." Another says:

> When people are being promoted for being an 'SME [subject matter expert],' 'Top Analysis,' recognized expert,' 'my go to guy,' 'possesses unique knowledge,' all those are non-collaborative terms. But that's how people are promoted by management.... Although it was a unique situation with a very poor manager, when I was govie, I was fired from a leadership position on a small program because I collaborated too much. My manager told me that if everyone else knows this stuff, why do I need you? The problem is how can a manager measure collaboration? How does a manager determine who collaborates 'more' and deserves a promotion?

Obstacle Four: Practical Difficulties in Using the Tools

One person comments that asking questions on iSpace had never really resulted in good answers, and another comments that wikis are a pain to edit. "Overall, there are too many tools that are overly complicated and lack sufficient utility." Another cites the barriers to maintaining access. "When I do need or want something, my password or access has expired, and/ or I can't remember the separate passwords I'm required to have for those applications ... I have an Intellipedia page that I have let lapse because I can never remember the command/ syntax for changing things and don't have the time to experiment." One other person makes the same comment, specifically with regard to i-Space and Intellipedia.

Several respondents identify the lack of much guidance about which tool is best for which task. One enthusiast says it is still difficult to know whether the investment is worth what you get from it. "It is easy to find yourself feeding these tools for the sake of feeding them." Another comment was a slightly different take on that theme, applauding the tools but noting that there was no obvious place for them in the normal workflow. Another adds the point that the security modifications necessary to transfer tools to the CIA tend to make them "clunky at best and at worst data/server hogs that get in the way vice help." For another person, A-Space was a mistake, "a closed and more difficult version of Intellipedia [that] resulted directly in loss of critical collaborative mass."

NSA faces a special category of obstacles. It seeks to share as much as possible with its "five eyes" international partners—Britain, Canada, Australia and New Zealand. But Intelink on JWICS is NOFORN, which means it is inaccessible to non-Americans. As one NSAer says: "Why post on a system that eliminated some of their most important partners (commonwealth allies)?" Or, as another notes: "NSA was nearly prohibited from using the JWICS interface, and it was very difficult to get on. It's easier now, but it's still too damn hard. And it's slower than NSANet, and who has time to figure these things out when we're not entirely sure what benefit there is."

Promising Initiatives in Collaboration

CollabZones was featured in the introduction. Two other initiatives are worth noting. One, Living Intelligence, is collaborative but still mostly on the drawing boards. The other is a collaboration architecture but one as yet confined *within* an agency, NSA.

A team at NGA produced Living Intelligence as a prototype, one that aims to merge the virtues of crowdsourcing with agency vetting, and to reduce duplication in the process.[29] It would transform both the production and the "consumption" of intelligence. Unlike CollabZones, it remains for now in the "intriguing idea" category. It would use Google Living Story software, software developed for a 2009–2011 experiment involving Google, the *New York Times* and *Washington Post*. Every topic would have its own URL. At the top of the page for each "story" would be a summary, and below that a timeline, which the user could move back and forth. On the left side of the page, filters would let users drill down to the desired level of detail. On the right would be a time sequence of important events. In the center an update stream would keep track of the entire story. Once a user had read a piece, that piece would gray out, so the user need not read it again. The scheme would keep repetition to a medium, trying to distinguish between useful tailoring for different audiences and merely repeating the "stock" story.

---

29. For a video explaining the idea from the leader of the team, Chris Rasmussen, see http://www.youtube.com/watch?v=9ft3BBBg99 s&feature=plcp.

Finally, the content would be fully vetted by the contributing agencies, thus diminishing the worry that content on collaborative tools is second-rate or less reliable. The page would use grayed versus lit agency icons, plus color coding, to make clear which contributions to the topic had been vetted and cleared at which level of the contributing agencies. The software involved permits geospatial location, so the topic page would add a spatial dimension as well. The hope is that this form of collaboration would encourage agencies to play to their strengths, rather than try to do the entire story themselves.

NSA is developing a Tradecraft ECOsystem, driven by the needs of analysts and based on three inter-linked elements. Figure 5 displays the elements:

Figure 5: An Evolving NSA Collaboration Ecosystem

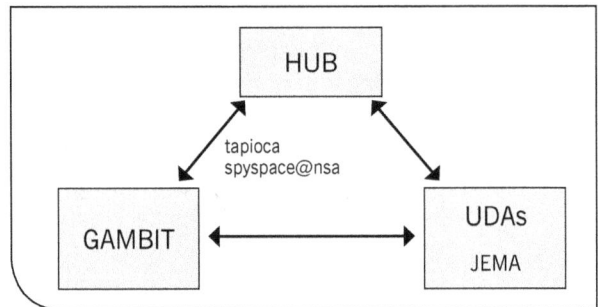

- HUB is the place analysts go to learn about the models and ideas available to them. It has a detailed explanation of how to use particular analytic methods and how to use existing capabilities. It aims to provide the answer to "How do I do x?"

- GAMBIT is somewhat like Stackoverflow, used by Starbucks and others to get suggestions. On GAMBIT, analysts can look for insights about how to do their jobs more efficiently, asking "Wouldn't it be cool if xyz could be done?" The query will go all across NSA's entire Analysis and Production Directorate, and may be passed to the Technology Directorate if a more corporate solution makes sense.

- UDAs, or User-Driven Analytics, like Kepler Project, ArcView or ModelBuilder, let users "drag and drop" code to do modeling in their own environment, as well as streamline or automate analytics.

- JEMA, or Joint Enterprise and Modeling Environment, is a component of UDA. It lets a user choose from literally thousands of models to plug-and-play with other analytics (or apps), somewhat like attaching Lego blocks together to create a unique piece (model). The most-used models get reviewed and validated by subject matter experts (SMEs). There are metrics to track and document the use of models.

Looking across the Intelligence Community, while the *internal* IM tools, like SameTime, are used the most, some officers find value in the cross-agency tools, and sometimes use the internal and cross-agency tools in combination—for instance, asking questions on SameTime, then posting answers on Intellipedia.

The obstacles to using the collaborative tools can be classified into three clusters, in ascending order of importance. First, classification issues are most visible in NSA's isolation from Intelink because the latter is NOFORN. But bloggers on the classified or "high" side have to upload unclassified documents they'd like readers to see. Second, the tools are perceived as clunky and hard to use, requiring multiple passwords and knowledge of special syntax. Third, and most important, are disincentives of various kinds, ranging from trust to the lack of incentives. Ultimately, as the blogger puts it: "our work processes are linear and hierarchical, rather than group-collaborative. That is especially true across agency boundaries—genuine cross-agency collaboration remains relatively rare."

Findings and Recommendations

Overall, the agencies and the Intelligence Community have spawned an impressive array of collaborative tools—"too many," some interlocutors complain. Yet most of those, like the SameTime example, are confined to collaboration *within* agencies, not across them, and are used mostly for peer-to-peer communication, thus not widely "collaborative." So, too, in most cases the actual use of available cross-agency tools on Intelink is a tiny fraction of the potential usage. In some cases, though, when a tool fits a particular need, like Inteldocs, use rises impressively. Moreover, it is difficult to track whether collaborative discussions on these tools make any difference to the ultimate quality of intelligence products or decisions—a challenge the private sector faces as well.

A constant in all the conversations is the relationship between collaboration as enabled by new tools, on the one hand, and the traditional processes for producing finished intelligence, on the other. The enthusiasts hoped that new forms of collaboration would supplant the traditional processes for producing finished intelligence. However, that goal will remain elusive *so long as finished intelligence retains its dominant current form—stovepiped, branded words on paper or bytes on a screen.* Yet what is called "finished intelligence" will also change, and that will open new possibilities for collaborative tools, perhaps over a longer time frame. For now, the challenge for the DNI and other intelligence leaders is to take a more strategic view of new forms of collaboration: how far to push that strategic view depends on what the traffic will bear and how much, how soon, those traditional processes change. The paper concludes with a range of possible steps in taking a strategic view, from exhortation to example to incentives.

Findings

Surveying the IC's practices in tool-facilitated collaboration reveals the importance of organizational culture, incentives, and professional development, as reflected in the findings below.

Finding One: Organizational Culture Matters in the Use of Collaborative Tools

In many respects, social media and intelligence are polar opposites. The latter is closed and passive; the former are transparent and active. The temptation for intelligence officers to "just say no" to participating in *external* social media, like Facebook, is understandable if perhaps unwise (if 20-somethings disappear from social media when they join intelligence agencies, they become "conspicuous by their absence," almost advertising their new affiliation). That attitude seems to wash over internal collaborative tools as well as external ones. Even if the concerns over operational security are far less present with internal tools, the organizational culture, especially in several of the agencies, does not extend the circle of trust beyond agency lines, if that far. In some cases, the resistance reflects the desire of younger officers to separate their professional from their personal lives. And the interviews suggest that younger officers can be quickly socialized into the traditional processes.

Finding Two: Incentives Matter in the Use of Collaborative Tools

Currently, a great deal of participation in collaborative tools is viewed as wasting time, all the more so because that participation is disconnected from traditional production. Frequent users of collaborative tools believe they pay a price for doing so. Recall the CIA officer who called himself "pretty much unpromotable." Part of taking a more strategic view of collaboration and collaborative tools will be deciding how, and how much, to reward officers for collaboration, like blogs, that is not directly relevant to immediate production. Shifting the culture to empower users to contribute and feel free to collaborate will require changes in incentives.

Finding Three: Reputation of Individual Collaborators Encourages Collaboration

A reputation for being a collaborative tools enthusiast can be a negative, especially when it comes to performance appraisal and promotion. Generating a positive reputation is something of an unnatural act for intelligence officers, many of whom work hard to ensure that their names are not widely known on the outside. Trying to get their name known widely on the inside thus cuts against the grain. NSA's experience with Tapioca is telling in that regard. "Ambassadors" for Tapioca can be given kudos for their work. Initially, the kudos were private, and the recipients had to act to make them public. They didn't, so public became the default option, with officers needing to take action to keep the kudos private. Tapioca's managers judged the "liking" process of Facebook as offensive to the agency's culture, but they still wanted some way of ranking both an officer's domains of expertise and answers to questions. In both cases, the expertise of the ranker is weighted in the ranking, and more highly ranked answers appear brighter than less highly ranked ones.

Finding Four: Too Many Tools Discourages Collaboration

Many interviewees believe the Community suffers from a surfeit of tools, the legacy of the "let a thousand flowers bloom" period irrigated with plenty of money for seedlings. Some people report being unsure, as a result, where to participate. One CIA analyst suggests that if an officer is tempted to blog, he or she might start close to home, on the internal CIA blog. If that posting brought only a tepid response, then the officer would either stop blogging altogether, or try the Intelink blog. A DIA officer had a logical solution to the "where to participate?" issue. He registered for every tool that arose but only with just enough information to guide others to his "home page" on Intellipedia.

The survey responses from non-users include many comments about the practical difficulties of using the tools for harried officials. Those difficulties weighed heavily in the implicit calculation of whether it was worth the trouble, only compounding the perceived risk that arises in collaborating—but not in *not* collaborating. Moreover, the current access rules raise what is called the "all-all" problem: when officers seek information in a collaborative platform, the way they ensure they don't miss anything is to check "all regions" and "all issues," never mind whether or not they have a need to know about all of them.

Finding Five: The Use of Collaborative Tools Can Reveal Different Perspectives

The "discovery" role of unplanned collaboration through social media does bring together different perspectives, ones that couldn't be gotten from just those in the same office or field. This theme runs through many of our conversations, though it is difficult to validate from the available data. Even when collaborative tools connect two analysts in different agencies working on the same account, almost by definition the two will find a new perspective simply because the other analyst previously was unknown.

Finding Six: Collaborative Tools Contribute to Professional Development

Social media might also play a role in professional development. Attending a conference, for instance, is aimed at discovering new expertise, ideas, methods, and conceptual frameworks. One official blogs regularly about conferences he attends, thus spreading the discovery and interaction to previously unknown peers in the Intelligence Community. Blogging might be thought of and managed as a set of ongoing "virtual conferences." The emphasis on professional development varies widely across the Community, but to the extent that it is encouraged—which does not generally seem to be the case given the emphasis on responding to questions from consumers first—social media participation could be viewed as a form of professional development. However, the Community first needs to decide the prior issue—how valuable explicit (as opposed to on-the-job) professional development is and how much it needs to be nurtured—before it explores the use of social media for this purpose.

Recommendations

The principal recommendation is that the DNI and agency leaders should take a more strategic view of collaboration and collaborative tools from the perspective of the Community enterprise. While a major reshaping of the Community's IT architecture—ICITE, for Intelligence Community Information Technology Enterprise—will in principle provide a common desktop environment across the Community, with shared applications, that initiative has yet to translate into a central framework for or much attention by agency seniors to what kinds of incentives to provide for what kinds of collaboration. Such a strategic view might conclude that a continuation of the current bottom-up, decentralized approach is fine, at least until the nature of intelligence production changes. The challenge of overcoming existing work cultures is, if anything, sharper for the Community than for private enterprises. For the DNI to produce a more strategic view will require taking some of the following steps, organized around the three obstacles identified earlier—classification, practical difficulties in using the tools, and, above all, incentives.

Recommendation One: Make Access to Collaborative Tools Easier

The challenge is to make the tools easier to get to and to use without increasing the risk officers perceive from using them or the "all, all" problem. From the ODNI's perspective, identity and access management are critical. The goal is a "persistent dynamic profile" that will let officers move easily from content, to collaboration to social media, very much paralleling the charts that move from peer-to-peer communication, to more collaborative tools, to collaborating to actually produce intelligence or another product—from "discourse" collaboration to "structured" collaboration. Here, the security walls of the Community might be an advantage: While the private sector seeks to exercise some control over collaboration even as it encourages it, the Intelligence Community has quite absolute control. It can know and track exactly what happens across collaborative tools.

Recommendation Two: Reshape IT Investments to Use Shared Platforms

Improving the classification part of the access problem—for instance, addressing the NOFORN restrictions—will be, to a considerable extent, hostage to the wider IT reshaping in the Community. Whatever the motivation to collaborate, the underlying IT will still be a limiting factor in acting on that interest, and the extent to which systems facilitate physical sharing of data may also encourage collaboration. Ironically, budgetary stringency may produce what years of exhortation and large budgets could not—sharing of platforms and, with it, easier sharing of information across agencies. ICITE (pronounced "eyesight") is driven by the need for budget reductions, and the goal is reducing total IT spending for the intelligence agencies by a quarter within five years, mostly through lower labor costs and bulk prices for software and hardware.[30] The fast (and most security-sensitive) horses, NSA and CIA, have responsibility for the cloud and for analytics, while DIA and NGA will develop a common desktop, or DTE (desktop environment). A common set of tools—called the Ozone Widget Framework—will be used to develop applications, which will then be made available through an NSA-managed "apps mall." Encryption and data tagging will allow for secure information sharing.

The process is being driven by the ODNI CIO, but a high-level Mission Users Group (MUG) is watching the process from the users' perspective. It has sorted IT needs into three bins:

- The huge apps, like e-mail, simply should be done jointly across the Community.

- The other extreme, the apps mall, probably should be driven by the particular needs of small groups of users.

- In between, the MUG has identified seven mission threads—important, hard intelligence issues like Pakistani nuclear weapons—which they are in effect using to stress test the emerging ICITE.

If ICITE in the context of declining budgets might push collaboration in ways that relative riches have not, there is also the risk of the opposite. If the savings from the move to the cloud do not materialize, and, simultaneously, budget stringency pushes agencies back toward what they regard as their core missions, inter-agency collaboration, and the tools to support it could come to be seen as luxuries. There will be pressure on the discretionary funding the DNI has to, say, support Intelink even as it is managed by NSA. In tackling these issues, modest investments in analytics would be valuable if the ODNI wants to determine which tools are the most useful, and more importantly perhaps, the most used. The road to a more sensible, useful, and collaborative toolkit for Intelligence Community analysts will be much shorter if better metrics pave the way

Recommendation Three: Take Practical Steps to Increase the Use of Tools

Create a Common Look and Feel. A more strategic and centralized view of tools, along with the reshaping of IT, should at least address the irksome obstacles of passwords and syntax. All of us suffer from far too many passwords in our daily life; for us the unsatisfactory answer is one from which intelligence officers are enjoined: we simply write them down. It should be possible, though, to let officers use their agency passwords for cross-agency tools, and to avoid several levels of passwords for access, especially those involving one level that is held by the tool managers. A common look and feel to the tools would also help, as would whatever can be done to use the same syntax or form for editing/blogging and the like across tools.

Require Training in the Tool, Including for Senior Officers. Most of the tools come with courses in how to use them, but taking the course is voluntary, depending on the initiative of individual officers. One Intellipedia manager's card lists his title as "Intellipedia Evangelist." The language is provocative but telling, implying that the tool requires an evangelist to spread the faith. Each agency is now required to have a course on community collaboration, so a starting point would be to include some basic training in how to use a few of the Community-wide collaborative tools, then to require more senior officers to take at least a few hours of such training.

---

30. See John Foley, "Intelligence Agencies Must Operate More Like an Enterprise," *Information Week,* January 14, 2013, available as of May 1, 2013 at http://www.informationweek.com/government/leadership/intelligence-agencies-must-operate-more/240146055.

Recommendation Four: Signal the Importance of Collaboration from Top Leadership

Set an Example. Even when agency seniors bless the use of collaborative tools, usually tepidly, they seldom actually *use* them. The NIC vice chair came up in our conversations as an exception, both blogging and responding to blogs. The CIA contrarian Red Cell uses blogs. Surely, little can be more powerful than the pull of example. For senior agency staff to set that example would make a difference—at relatively low cost.

Require Officers to Register. One suggestion is worth considering: requiring all Community officers to register for, say, three of the Community-wide tools. No one would be required to actually *use* the tools, but registering would ensure at least some passing familiarity with them. Which three would require some analysis of current usage. It would also require keeping a close eye on tool development outside the Community lest intelligence find itself five years hence having settled on three long-outmoded tools. The official who made this suggestion is an analyst, so his candidates were eChirp, Intellipedia and A-Space, the first for situational awareness, the second because it operates across levels of classification, and the third because it could include material at the HCS and G levels. Requiring registration might also be a way to decide which, if any, tools should be eliminated by letting officers vote with their registrations.

Use a Range of Incentives to Encourage Collaboration. Because coordination is required but collaboration is not, incentives for collaboration are weak. That culture will not change until the incentives do. The possible changes run from exhortation to promotion. At the lesser extreme, DNIs might explicitly recognize the value of collaboration not directly connected to finished products, and encourage other managers to do the same.

A next step would be to recognize—and again encourage other managers to recognize—the value of analysts and other officials spending some portion of their day blogging and collaborating in other forums, not necessarily connected to imminent production of finished intelligence. Ultimately, these forms of collaboration might be explicitly included in the performance appraisal process. A draft ODNI directive would include KSAs (knowledge, skills and aptitude) for "collaborative tradecraft" as part of those appraisals. Doing so would require creativity in creating some metrics and caution in applying them lest officers game the system—for instance, if making new connections were rewarded, the result could become a kind of LinkedIn behind the firewall, many but mostly meaningless contacts. But, somewhat on the model of the *New York Times*, finished intelligence might come with explicit mention of collaborators useful in its production, with those collaborators then rewarded in their performance appraisals.

Rewards might include monetary incentives—though budgetary travails make that difficult now—but money and even promotions don't drive most intelligence officials; if those rewards did drive them, they'd be on Wall Street. Rather promotions are valued less for the money they carry than for the recognition of having done a good job, respect among one's peers, and mission advantage by various metrics—writing items for the President's Daily Brief (PDB), finding Zawahiri, or recruiting a terrific asset. If people discovered that collaboration helped advance their mission, they'd be more tempted to collaborate.

Recommendation Five: Create a Shared Platform for Finished Intelligence

One variant of this idea would not change current production processes for finished intelligence but would require every agency to send its products to a central site, one managed by the ODNI. There, assessments on the same topic would be bundled together to provide one-stop shopping for consumers and intelligence officers alike. The next step would be to add a summary of similar points and differences, then let readers drill down a level if they sought a particular agency's view. If existing production processes remained intact, this would not only

What Civilian Agencies Can Learn from the Intelligence Community

Civilian agencies can learn from both what the Community can do in using collaborative tools and from what it so far hasn't done or finds difficult. Perhaps the most important lesson is that while collaboration has to bubble up from officials who see value in it, a push from the top is also imperative. If agency leaders think increasing collaboration is valuable, both within the agency and across agencies, they need to promote it and to set an example, by using available blogs, for instance. Those leaders need to set a strategic framework for collaboration.

Civilian agencies have more scope than intelligence agencies to leverage "external" tools for "internal" purpose, as MITRE did in building tools for DHS. Crowdsourcing to find answers for agency problems, or using Twitter and its kin to do outreach and manage crises, are both valuable. But taking the next step and opening "internal" communications to some set of interested outsiders can add both valuable perspectives and continuous assessments.

The Community's experience underscores that, in the end, collaboration has to be real—that is, integral to the agency's work processes. Many civilian agencies have less defined and visible products than the CIA's finished intelligence. But unless collaboration is an integral part of producing the agency's outputs, it will be limited to communities of interest. As the *New York Times* example suggests, if collaboration is to be real, the agency's ultimate product or output has to be collaborative.

provide for one-stop shopping but might also demonstrate the value of collaboration by displaying similarities and differences across agencies. Unfortunately, a version of this idea, called Intelligence Today, was tried in the second half of the 2000s and failed, for reasons not far to seek. Which agency would get top billing was contentious, and the exercise also became labor-intensive, so all agencies resisted contributing analysts to it. In the end, the DNI made the CIA the executive agent for the project, and the project died within a year. It is worth another try.

Living Intelligence is a more dramatic variant of this idea, one that would change both the way intelligence in produced and the way it is consumed. It is a harbinger of a broader change that is sweeping over intelligence, a shift from products toward services, from transactions toward relationships.[31] Intelligence is increasingly in the client service business, not the production of finished intelligence business. That realization is probably most taken at NGA, many of whose traditional products can now be bought commercially. It has the least purchase at the CIA, where the culture of finished intelligence is strongest. INR and DIA are in between; for the former, service is a fact of geography, sitting in the same building with its clients. Already, the PDB briefers are exemplars of the new role; interviews with principals found that while the principals interviewed like the document, they liked the briefers more. That role is especially evident in the longer conversations the president has with analysts, often several from different agencies who collaborated in producing the background paper.

By the same token, while national intelligence officers are also thought of as producers, they are probably more important as conversation partners and advice givers for policy counterparts. The Intelligence Community will continue to produce finished products for a long time to come. But if fostering collaboration should be near the top of the DNI's to-do list, beginning to think about how to take a more strategic view of production-cum-client-service should be on that list as well.

---

31.   See, for instance, Josh Kerbel and Anthony Olcott, "Synthesizing with Clients, Not Analyzing for Customers," *Studies in Intelligence*, 54, 4 (December 2010). For the reflections along similar lines of a wonderful group of analysts Treverton had the opportunity to organize, see "Products or Outputs? Probing the Implications of Changing the Outputs of Intelligence: A Report of the 2011 Analyst-IC Associate Teams Program," *Studies in Intelligence*, 56, 1 (March 2012).

Appendix: Basic Survey Instrument

- Do you use collaborative tools? If so, which? (Listed, depending on the agency: SameTime, Jabber, eChirp, Intelink blog, Intellipedia, A-Space)
  — Never
  — Tried a time or two and stopped
  — Once in a while
  — Often
  — Daily

- If so, what for?
  — Communicating with colleagues
  — General situation awareness
  — Finding colleagues or fellow experts
  — Seeking answers to questions
  — Putting down ideas for later use
  — Seeking comments on evolving ideas

- Do you consider yourself a passive or an active user of social media at work?
  — Completely passive (i.e., only read)
  — Somewhat active (e.g., comment on blogs)
  — Active (e.g., post in microblogs and blogs)
  — Very active (e.g., maintain a blog and initiate discussion streams in eChirp)

- If not, why not?
  — E-mail is fine
  — No time for tools
  — Don't see value in them
  — No professional or career incentive to use them

- Do you use social media in your non-work life?

- How long have you been at your agency?
  — Less than two years
  — Two to five years
  — Five to 10 years
  — More than 10 years

- If you do use the tools, can you cite specific examples of where they were especially helpful (or not)?

- Any other comments or suggestions?

References

Allen, Thomas J., *Managing the Flow of Technology* (Cambridge: MIT Press, 1977).

Amabile, Teresa, M., Chelly Patterson, Jennifer Mueller, Tom Wojcik, Steven J. Kramer, Paul W. Odomirok, and Mel Marsh, "Academic-Practitioner Collaboration in Management Research: A Case of Cross-Profession Collaboration," *Academy of Management Journal,* Vol. 44, No. 2, 2001, pp. 418–431.

Bercovici, Jeff "Who Coined 'Social Media? Web Pioneers Compete for Credit," *Forbes*, 09 December 2010, accessed 08 March 8, 2013 (http://www.forbes.com/sites/jeffbercovici/ 2010/12/09/who-coined-social-media-web-pioneers-compete-for-credit/).

Baldwin, Carliss Y., and Kim B. Clark, "Where Do Transactions Come From? A Network Design Perspective on the Theory of the Firm" (Working Paper, 2006).

Bjork, Bo-Christer, and David Solomon, "Open Access versus Subscription Journals: A Comparison of Scientific Impact," *BioMed Central Medicine,* Vol. 10, July 17, 2012. http://www.biomedcentral.com/1741-7015/10/73.

Brown, John S. and Paul Duguid, "Knowledge and Organization: A Social-Practice Perspective," *Organization Science* 12 (2001):206.

Buchanan, Matt, "There's Less 'Dark Social' than Meets the Eye," in *FWD*: BuzzFeed, 2012. As of October 30, 2012: http://www.buzzfeed.com/mattbuchanan/theres-less-dark-social-than-meets-the-eye.

Buchanan, Matt, "Where Did All The Email Sharing Go?" in *FWD*: BuzzFeed, 2012. As of October 30, 2012: http://www.buzzfeed.com/mattbuchanan/email-dies-a-little-bit-more

Bughin, Jacques and Michael Chui, "Evolution of the Networked Enterprise: Survey Results" McKinsey Global Survey Results, 2013. Accessed July 10, 2013 http://www.mckinsey.com/ insights/business_technology/evolution_of_the_networked_enterprise_mckinsey_global_survey_ results.

Bukvova, Helena, "Studying Research Collaboration: A Literature Review," *Sprouts: Working Papers on Information Systems*, Vol. 10, No. 3, 2010. http://sprouts.aisnet.org/10-3.

Burt, Ronald, *Structural Holes* (Cambridge: Harvard University Press, 1992).

Cain, Susan, *Quiet: The Power of Introverts in a World That Can't Stop Talking* (New York: Crown Publishers, 2012).

Chesbrough, Henry with James Euchner, "The Evolution of Open Innovation: An Interview with Henry Chesbrough," *Research Technology Management*, September–October, 2011.

Chui, Michael, and others. "The Social Economy: Unlocking Value and Productivity through Social Technologies," Report by the McKinsey Global Institute, July 2012.

Crozier, Michael, *The Bureaucratic Phenomenon* (Chicago: University of Chicago Press, 1964), 194.

Dahl, Allison, Jill Lawrence, and Jeff Pierce, "Building an Innovation Community," *Research Technology Management*, September–October 2011, 19–27.

Donaldson, Bill, Bala Iyer, Donna Cuomo, and Salvatore Parise, "Mitre Corporation: Using Social Technologies to Get Connected," *Ivey Business Journal,* Strategy, January/February 2011.

Drapeau, Mark and Linton Wells II, *Social Software and National Security: An Initial Net Assessment,* (Washington: Center for Technology and National Security Policy, National Defense University, April 2009, available as of 21 August 2013 at http://www.ndu.edu/ctnsp/Def_Tech/DTP61_SocialSoftwareandNationalSecurity.pdf.

duBruyn, Jason, "Duke Study: Spending on Social Media Marketing will Surge," *Triangle BizBlog,* February 26, 2013, available, as of April 5, 2013, at http://www.bizjournals.com/triangle/blog/2013/02/duke-study-spending-on-social-media.html?page=all.

Duggan, Maeve and Joanna Brenner, "The Demographics of Social Media Users—2012," Pew Research Center, 14 February 2013, accessed on 09 March 2013 (http://pewinternet.org/~/media//Files/Reports/2013/PIP_SocialMediaUsers.pdf).

Enserink, Martin, "As Open Access Explodes, How to Tell the Good From the Bad and the Ugly," *Science,* Vol. 338, November 23, 2012.

"Evolution of the Networked Enterprise: McKinsey Global Survey Results," March 2013, available as of April 3, 2013, https://www.mckinseyquarterly.com/article_print.aspx?L2=4&L3=43&ar=3073, as of August 20, 2013.

Fishkin, Rand, "Testing the Accuracy of Visitor Data from Alexa, Compete, Google Trends, Doubleclick & Quantcast," in *The Daily SEO Blog*: SEOmoz, 2012. As of November 6, 2012: http://www.seomoz.org/blog/testing-accuracy-visitor-data-alexa-compete-google-trends-quantcast.

Fleming, Lee and David M. Waguespack, "Brokerage, Boundary Spanning, and Leadership in Open Innovation Communities," *Organization Science* 18 (2007):166.

Foley, John, "Intelligence Agencies Must Operate More like an Enterprise," *Information Week,* January 14, 2013, available as of May 1, 2013 at http://www.informationweek.com/government/leadership/intelligence-agencies-must-operate-more/240146055.

Ganter, John H., "Collaborative Situational Awareness: How a Cross-Cultural Chat Room Encourages Intelligence Sharing during Counterproliferation Operations," Sandia National Laboratories, 2011-0114J, March 2011.

Gibson, Cristina B. and Jennifer L. Gibbs, "Unpacking the Concept of Virtuality: The effects of geographic dispersion, electronic dependence, dynamic structure, and national diversity on team innovation," *Administrative Science Quarterly* 51 (2006):451–495.

Hackman, Richard J., *Collaborative Intelligence: Using Teams to Solve Hard Problems*, San Francisco: Berrett-Koehler, 2011.

Hansen, Morton T., *Collaboration: How Leaders Avoid the Traps, Create Unity, and Reap Big Results*, Boston: Harvard Business School Publishing, 2009.

Hartman, Joshua and Kevin J. Resch, *The Future of Commercial GEOINT Services: A Look at Where We Have Been and Where We Are Going,* (np;_The Center for Strategic Space Studies, September 2011), pp. 1–2.

Hayden, Beth and Rafal Tomal, "A History of Social Media [Infographic]," *Copyblogger*, accessed 08 March 8, 2013 (http://www.copyblogger.com/history-of-social-media/#more-29103).

Ingram, Mathew, "Dark Social: Why Measuring User Engagement is Even Harder Than You Think," GigaOM, 2012. As of November 6, 2012: http://gigaom.com/2012/10/12/dark-social-why-measuring-user-engagement-is-even-harder-than-you-think/.

Kaplan, Andreas M. and Michael Haenlein, "Users of the World, Unite! The Challenges and Opportunities of Social Media," *Business Horizons*, 53, 59–68, 2010.

Kerbel, Josh, and Anthony Olcott, "Synthesizing with Clients, Not Analyzing for Customers," *Studies in Intelligence*, 54, 4 (December 2010).

Laakso, Mikael, and Bo-Christer Bjork, "Anatomy of Open Access Publishing: A Study of Longitudinal Development and Internal Structure," *BioMed Central Medicine,* Vol. 10, No. 124, October 22, 2012: http://www.biomedcentral.com/1741-7015/10/124.

Larcker, David F., Sarah M. Larcker and Brian Tayan, "What Do Corporate Directors and Senior Managers Know about Social Media?" *The Conference Board*, No. DN-V4N20, October 2012, accessed 09 March 2013 (http://www.gsb.stanford.edu/sites/default/files/documents/TCB_DN-V4N20-12.Social_Media.pdf).

Lenhart, Amanda, "Teens, Smartphones & Texting," Pew Internet & American Life Project, March 19, 2012, 2012. As of November 1, 2012: http://pewinternet.org/~/media//Files/Reports/2012/PIP_Teens_Smartphones_and_Texting.pdf.

Lesser, Eric L., Michael A. Fontaine, and Jason A. Slusher, *Knowledge and Communities*, Woburn: Butterworth-Heinemann, 2012.

Lesser, E. L., and J. Storck, "Communities of Practice and Organizational Performance," *IBM Systems Journal,* Vol. 40, No. 4, 2001, pp. 831–841.

Lupfer, Elizabeth, "Dell Uses Social Media to Foster Employee Ideas and Engagement," *The Social Workplace*, 02 October 2009, accessed on 10 March 2013 (http://www.thesocial-workplace.com/2009/10/02/dell-uses-social-media-to-foster-employee-ideas-and-engage-ment/).

Madrigal, Alexis, "Dark Social: We Have the Whole History of the Web Wrong," in *Technology*: The Atlantic, 2012. As of October 30, 2012: http://www.theatlantic.com/technology/archive/2012/10/dark-social-we-have-the-whole-history-of-the-web-wrong/263523/.

McAfee, Andrew, *Enterprise 2.0: New Collaborative Tools for Your Organization's Toughest Challenges* (Boston: Harvard Business Press, 2009), p. 126.

Miller, Rohn Jay, "Dark Social? Are Our Analytics Missing Hugh Chunks of Social Traffic?" socialmediatoday, 2012. As of October 17. 2012: http://socialmediatoday.com/rohnjaymiller/918061/dark-social-are-our-analytics-missing-huge-chunks-social-traffic.

Mitchell, Amy, Tom Rosenstiel, Laura Houston Santhanam, and Leah Christian, "Future of Mobile News: The Explosion in Mobile Audiences and a Close Look at What It Means for News," Journalism.org: Pew Research Center's Project for Excellence in Journalism, 2012. As of November 1, 2012: http://www.journalism.org/analysis_report/future_mobile_news.

Morgan, Jacob, "The Impact of Collaboration on Enterprise Business Performance," 2010. As of October 22: http://www.jmorganmarketing.com/the-impact-of-collaboration-on-enterprise-business-performance/.

Nicholas, David, and Ian Rowlands, "Social Media Use in the Research Workflow," Information Services & Use 31 (2011) 61–83.

Polanyi, Michael, The Tacit Dimension (Gloucester, MA: Peter Smith, 1983).

"Products or Outputs? Probing the Implications of Changing the Outputs of Intelligence: A Report of the 2011 Analyst-IC Associate Teams Program," Studies in Intelligence, 56, 1 (March 2012).

Office of the Director of National Intelligence, 2012 Annual Report on Security Clearance Determinations, (Washington: ODNI, 2013), available, as of October 22, 2013, at http://www.dni.gov/files/documents/2012%20Report%20on%20Security%20Clearance%20Determinations%20Final.pdf

O'Reilly Radar blog's "Four Short Links" (e.g., http://radar.oreilly.com/2013/06/four-short-links-3-june-2013.html).

Rosenberg, Nathan, Inside the Black Box: Technology and Economics (New York: Cambridge University Press, 1982).

Rosenstiel, Tom, and Amy Mitchell, The Future of Mobile News: The Explosion in Mobile Audiences and a Close Look at What it Means for You, Pew Research Center Project for Excellence in Journalism, October 1, 2012. As of November 1, 2012: http://www.journalism.org/sites/journalism.org/files/Futureofmobilenews%20_final1.pdf.

Ruppel, Kellsey, "The History of Oracle Connect," Oracle WebCenter Blog 13 February 2012, accessed on 10 March 2013, https://blogs.oracle.com/webcenter/entry/the_history_of_oracle_connect.

Sammons, Stephanie, "Five Tips for Effectively Managing a LinkedIn Group," Social Media Examiner, accessed 20 March 2013 (http://www.socialmediaexaminer.com/managing-linke-din-groups/).

Shaughnessy, Hayden, "Dark Social 2: How a Big Assumption of Social Media is Just Plain Wrong," in Tech: Forbes, 2012. As of November 6, 2012: http://www.forbes.com/sites/haydn-shaughnessy/2012/10/17/dark-social-2-how-a-big-assumption-of-social-media-is-just-plain-wrong/.

"Social Media," Wikipedia, accessed 09 March 2013: http://en.wikipedia.org/wiki/Social_media.

Sonderman, Jeff, "Survey: Americans Turn to Established Media for Breaking News, Mobile," Media News: Poynter, 2012. As of October 30, 2012: http://www.poynter.org/latest-news/top-stories/190586/new-data-show-shifting-patterns-as-people-seek-news-across-platforms/.

Sonderman, Jeff, "Pew: After Email, Getting News is the Most Popular Activity on Smartphones, Tablets," in Media News: Poynter, 2012. As of November 6, 2012: http://www.poynter.org/latest-news/media-lab/mobile-media/189899/pew-after-email-getting-news-is-the-second-most-popular-activity-on-smartphone-tablets/.

Spotlight: Definition of Collaborative Tools, Collaborative Tools Strategy, University of California, Berkeley, March 2009, accessed 09 March 2013: http://technology.berkeley.edu/cio/presentations/ucbcts/ucbcts_spotlight-definition_collaborative_tools.pdf.

Sonnenwald, Diane H., "Scientific Collaboration," *Annual Review of Information Science and Technology,* Vol. 41, No. 1, 2007, pp. 643–681, accessed 21 August 2013: http://dx.doi.org/10.1002/aris.2007.1440410121.

Surowiecki, James. "The Wisdom of Crowds: Why the Many Are Smarter Than the Few and How Collective Wisdom Shapes Business." *Economies, Societies and Nations* (2004).

Takada, Kouhei, Koshitaka Sakurai, Rainer Knauf Kinshuk, and Setsuo Tsurata, "Enriched Cyberspace Through Adaptive Multimedia Utilization for Dependable Remote Collaboration," *IEEE Transactions on Systems, Man, and Cybernetics—Part A: Systems and Humans,* Vol. 42, No. 5, September, 2012, pp. 1026–1039.

Thomson, Ann Marie, James L. Perry, and Theodore K. Miller, "Conceptualizing and Measuring Collaboration," *Journal of Public Administration Research and Theory,* Vol. 19, No. 1, 2009, pp. 23–56.

Treverton, Gregory F., *The "First Callers": The President's Daily Brief (PDB) across Three Administrations,* (Washington: Center for the Study of Intelligence, 2013), (document U/FOUO).

Tushman, Michael L., "Special Boundary Roles in the Innovation Process," *Administrative Science Quarterly* 22 (1977):587–605.

Von Hippel, Eric, "Sticky Information and the Locus of Problem-Solving: Implications for Innovation," *Management Science* 40 (1994):429–439.

"Web 2.0," Wikipedia, accessed 27 March 2013: http://en.wikipedia.org/wiki/Web_2.0.

"What is Usenet?" www.usenet.net, accessed 08 March 2013 (http://www.usenet.net/usenet-faq/#_usenet).

"What We Talk About When We Talk About 'Social,'" *Harvard Business Review*, accessed on 09 March 2013: http://blogs.hbr.org/cs/2013/02/what_we_talk_about_when_we_tal.html.

Wikipedia, *Collaboration,* http://en.wikipedia.org/wiki/Collaboration (as of October 24, 2012).

Yang, Tian-jian, "Financial Performance Analysis of E-collaboration Supply Chain under Transportation Disruptions," *Computer Science and Computational Technology, 2008.*

About the Author

Gregory F. Treverton is chairman of the U.S. National Intelligence Council (NIC). Earlier, he served in government on the first Senate Intelligence Committee, the National Security Council, and as vice chair of the NIC. He has been president of the Pacific Council of International Policy and director of studies at the International Institute for Strategic Studies in London. He has also held positions on the faculty of Harvard University's Kennedy School of Government and the School of International and Public Affairs at Columbia University.

Dr. Treverton's current research interests revolve around ways of thinking about the future, the increasing intersection of "public" and "private," and the role of social media in both collaboration and intelligence analysis. His books include *Covert Action: The Limits of Intervention in the Postwar World* (Basic Books, 1987); *America, Germany and the Future of Europe* (Princeton University Press, 1992); and *Rethinking America's Security*, edited with Graham T. Allison (Norton, 1992). His most recent books are *Reshaping National Intelligence for an Age of Information* (Cambridge University Press, 2003); *Intelligence for an Age of Terror* (Cambridge University Press, 2009); *Dividing Divided States* (University of Pennsylvania Press, 2014); and *National Intelligence and Science: Beyond the Great Divide in Analysis and Policy*, with Wilhelm Agrell (Oxford University Press, 2015). He is a member of the Council on Foreign Relations and the Swedish Royal Academy of War Science. He received his B.A. from Princeton University and his Ph.D. in public policy from Harvard University.

This report is the author's own work and does not reflect the views of the NIC, the director of national intelligence, the U.S. government, or CSIS.

www.ingramcontent.com/pod-product-compliance
Lightning Source LLC
Chambersburg PA
CBHW081437270326
41932CB00019B/3246